PROJECT SCIENCE

Materials

Written by Sally Hewitt

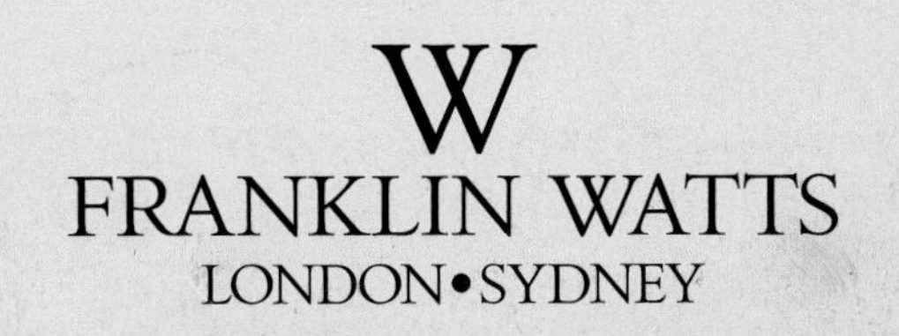

First published as *Starting Science: Materials* in 2009
by Franklin Watts. This edition 2012

338 Euston Road, London NW1 3BH

Franklin Watts Australia
Level 17/207 Kent Street, Sydney NSW 2000

Editor: Katie Dicker
Art Direction: Dibakar Acharjee (Q2AMedia)
Designer: Ritu Chopra (Q2AMedia)
Picture researcher: Kamal Kumar (Q2AMedia)
Craft models made by: Divij Singh (Q2AMedia)
Photography: Dibakar Acharjee (Q2AMedia)

Picture credits:
t=top b=bottom c=centre l=left r=right

Cover: Pending
Title page: Olga Lis/Shutterstock
Insides: Istockphoto: 6, Eugene Hoshiko/Associated Press: 7t, Vlad Turchenko/Dreamstime: 7b, Jupiter Images: 8bl, Jupiter Images: 8br, Jupiter Images: 9t, Stuart Miles/Shutterstock: 9bl, Svetoslav Iliev/Shutterstock: 9br, Antonio Munoz Palomares/Shutterstock: 10tr, Radius Images/Jupiter Images: 10bl, Brand New Images/Getty Images: 12tr, Imagesource/Photolibrary: 12bl, Vera Bogaerts/Shutterstock: 14, Bierchen/Shutterstock: 15tr, Susan Stewart/Istockphoto: 16, Florin Tirlea/Shutterstock: 17tr, Olga Lis/Shutterstock: 18bl, Harm Kruyshaar/Shutterstock: 18br, Shutterstock: 19tr, Danilo Ascione/Shutterstock: 19bl, David Rubinger/Corbis: 20, Maciej Mamro/Shutterstock: 21tr, Stok-Yard Studio/Jupiter Images: 21bl, Eliza Snow/Istockphoto: 22l, Filip Put/Istockphoto: 22r, Akira/Amanaimages/Corbis: 23tr, Alain Le Bot/Photononstop/Photolibrary: 24tr, Sylvain Grandadam/Photolibrary: 24bl, Martin Gnedt/Associated Press: 26, www.army.mil: 27tr, Pascal Goetgheluck/Science Photo Library: 27bl.
Q2AMedia Image Bank: Imprint page, Contents page, 11, 13, 15, 17, 19br, 21br, 23, 25.

With thanks to our model Shruti Aggarwal.

A CIP catalogue record for this book is available from the British Library

ISBN: 978 1 4451 0950 3

Dewey Classification: 620.1'1

Printed in China

Franklin Watts is a division of Hachette Children's Books, an Hachette UK company.
www.hachette.co.uk

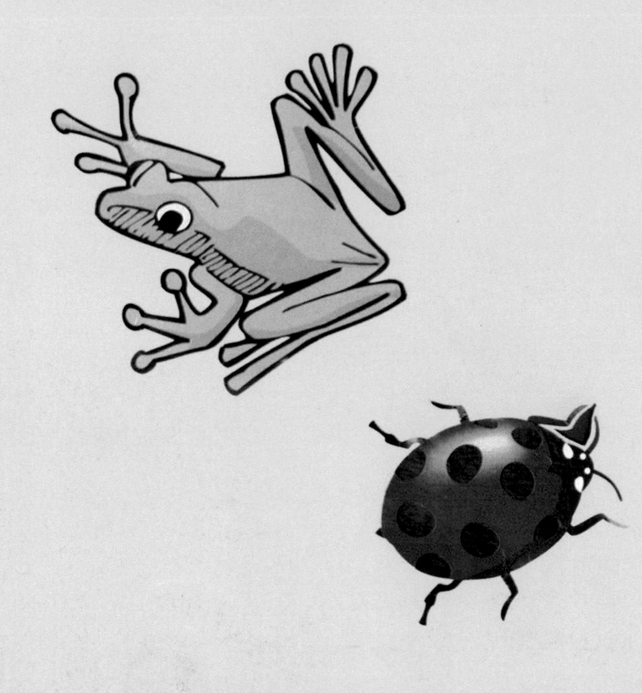

Contents

Words that appear in **bold** can be found in the glossary on pages 28–29.

What are materials?

Things that have been made, such as books and clothes and cars, all come from materials. Paper is the material used to make books, cotton to make shirts and metal to make cars.

Natural materials

Some materials are natural. They come from animals or plants or they are found in the ground. Wool comes from the soft coats of sheep, wood from the trunks of trees and marble is a kind of rock.

Wool comes from the soft coats of sheep. It is spun to make wool fibre.

Made materials

Some materials are made from other materials. Glass is a **mixture** of sand and **limestone** that has been heated. Plastic is made from oil. Paper is made from small chips of wood and water.

Brightly coloured toys are made from strong, light plastic in this toy factory.

Right for the job

Materials are chosen for the kind of job they have to do. Soft, warm wool is used to make winter coats and jumpers. Tough metal is used to make strong, long-lasting bridges.

This metal bridge is strong enough to carry traffic. It also bends without breaking in high winds.

What is a solid?

Materials come in three different forms: solid, liquid or gas. A solid is able to hold a shape. Some solid materials, such as wood or clay, can be cut or **moulded** to change their shape.

Weight and size

Solid objects can be light or heavy for their size, depending on the material they are made from. **Polystyrene foam**, for example, is full of air pockets. This makes it light to carry.

A big body board made of polystyrene (left) is lighter than a small bowling ball made from a heavy plastic (right).

Properties of materials

Solid materials have different qualities or **properties**. For example, they can be hard or soft, **waterproof** or **absorbent**, heavy or light, shiny or dull. These properties make them useful for a particular purpose.

A waterproof shower cap keeps your hair dry, while a soft towel absorbs the water.

Test the properties of solid materials

You will need:

- sponge • coin • sheet of plastic • lump of clay
- bowl of water

1 Press and squeeze the sponge, coin, plastic and clay to find out whether the materials are soft or hard.

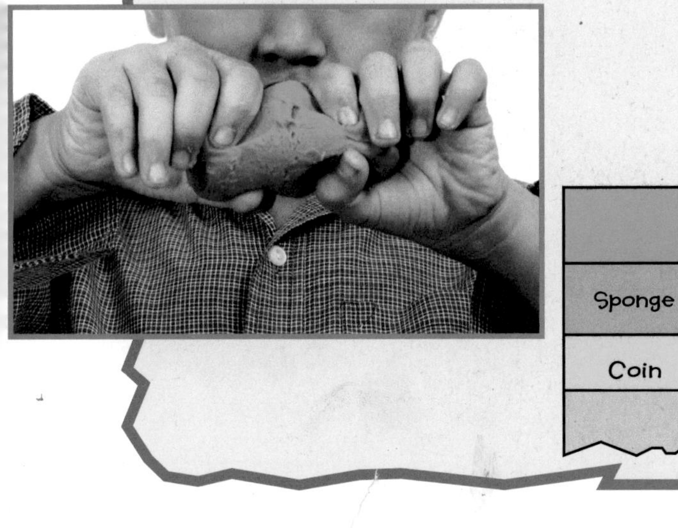

2 Put each material in the water to find out which materials float, sink, are waterproof or absorbent.

3 Make a chart like the one shown below to record your findings.

Materials float when they are light for their size. Materials that are heavy for their size are not supported by the water, and so they sink.

	Soft	Hard	Waterproof	Absorbent	Float	Sink
Sponge	✓			✓	✓	
Coin		✓				✓

What is a liquid?

Water, honey and oil are different kinds of liquid. Liquids flow and pour. Water flows out of a tap when you turn it on. River water pours over a cliff to make a waterfall.

No shape of its own

A liquid doesn't have a shape of its own. It takes the shape of whatever container it is in. If you spill your juice, it spreads out and makes a puddle!

When you pour juice into a glass, the liquid takes the shape of the glass.

Honey is a thick liquid so it drips slowly off this honey dipper.

Thick and thin

Some liquids are thicker than others and they flow differently. Thin liquids, such as water or milk, flow quickly and splash when you pour them. Thick liquids, such as honey and oil, pour slowly.

The great pouring race

You will need:

- 3 clear plastic cups
- honey • oil • washing-up liquid • ruler • sticky tape
- chopping board • pile of books
- washing-up bowl

1 Fill the cups by about a third (one with honey, one with oil and one with washing-up liquid).

2 Tape the cups firmly to a ruler (as shown above).

3 Lean the chopping board against some books and a washing-up bowl to make a slope.

4 Tip the ruler gently so the liquids start to pour out of the cups onto the top of the slope. Which liquid wins the pouring race?

You will find that the liquids move at different speeds down the slope. Thin liquids move quickly. Thick liquids take longer to reach the bottom of the slope.

What is a gas?

Gases are often difficult to see, smell or feel, but they are just as real as solids and liquids. The air around us is a mixture of gases. We breathe air in and out of our lungs.

Moving and flowing

Gases have no shape of their own. As they flow and move around, they spread to fill whatever container they are in. Gases can also be squashed to take up less space.

Air from your lungs squashes into a balloon when you blow it up.

Hot air makes this balloon rise. When the air cools, the balloon will sink back down to the ground.

Hot air

When air heats up, it **expands** or spreads out and becomes lighter than cold air. Lighter hot air rises above heavier, colder air.

Create a gas and make a volcano erupt

You will need:

- small plastic bottle • large tray • self-hardening clay
- waterproof paints and brush
- 50 g bicarbonate of soda
- jug with a mixture of 125 ml warm water, 60 ml washing-up liquid and a few drops of red food colouring
- 2 tablespoons of vinegar

1 Stand the empty bottle on the tray. Build a volcano shape around it with the clay, leaving the top of the bottle free. When the clay is dry, paint your volcano.

2 Put the bicarbonate of soda in the bottle and pour in the liquid mixture.

3 Now add some vinegar and stand back! Watch your volcano erupt.

When the vinegar and the bicarbonate of soda mix, they create bubbles of a gas called **carbon dioxide**, making it fizz up out of the volcano.

Water

Water can be a solid, a liquid or a gas. Ice is solid water. Liquid water is found in rivers, lakes and seas. An invisible gas called water vapour is in the air all around us.

Freezing point

Liquid water **freezes** into solid ice at 0°C. It stays frozen below that temperature, but will **melt** when the temperature rises above 0°C. An ice cube from the freezer, for example, quickly melts in your drink on a hot day.

In the summer, icebergs gradually melt as they float into warmer sea water.

Evaporation

When water is warmed by the Sun, it **evaporates** and turns into water vapour. Water vapour rises and cools into water droplets that form clouds. Water falls back to the Earth as rain, sleet or snow.

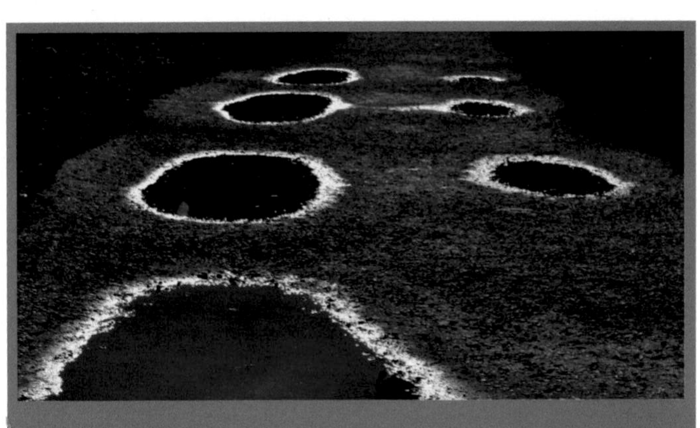

The rain water in these puddles disappears when it evaporates into water vapour.

Make a watery print

You will need:

- ice-cube tray • water
- food colouring
- absorbent paper (or a white cloth) • large tray

1 Fill an ice-cube tray with water.

2 Add a few drops of food colouring to some of the cubes and put the tray into a freezer.

3 When the cubes are frozen, put them on the paper on a large tray in the sunshine. Arrange them in a pretty shape or pattern.

As the ice cubes melt, the water will evaporate and leave a coloured watery pattern on the paper or cloth.

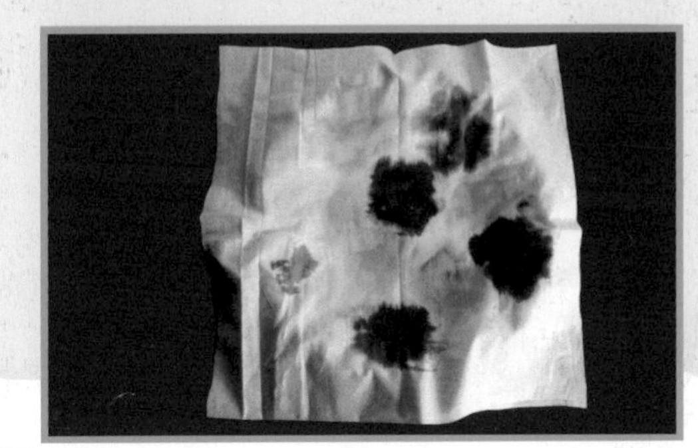

Mixtures and solutions

All kinds of things are mixtures. Sand is a mixture of broken rock and sea shells. Soil is a mixture of broken rock, dead animals and plants. Even muesli is a mixture of grains, nuts and fruit.

Solutions

Some things **dissolve** in water. This means they mix completely and make a **solution**. Sugar dissolves in a cup of hot tea. Salt dissolves in hot soup. You can't see the sugar or salt, but you can taste them.

Sea water is a solution of water and minerals. It tastes salty and is not good to drink!

Stalagmites and stalactites

Stalagmites and **stalactites** can be found in caves. They form when water drips off the cave roof onto the floor. Minerals dissolved in the water are left behind when the water evaporates. They create strange-shaped columns.

Stalagmites and stalactites take thousands of years to form.

Make a stalactite

You will need:

- 2 small jars • warm water
- bicarbonate of soda
- spoon • 2 lengths of wool (about 30 cm) • saucer or plate

1 Fill the jars with warm water. Gradually add and stir in as much soda as will dissolve to make a solution in each jar.

2 Place the saucer between the jars in a warm place [a sunny window-sill or a shelf above a radiator]. Twist the wool together and hang one end in each jar.

3 Leave for a few days. Watch crystals of soda form on the wool, drip onto the saucer and form a stalactite.

Heat

Heat changes materials. When metal becomes hot it expands. When paper and wood become very hot, they catch fire. Hot water **boils** and turns into water vapour.

Cooking

Cooking changes some foods in such a way that they can't be changed back again. When bread is toasted, it becomes harder and turns brown. Crunchy vegetables become soft. The white of an egg changes colour and becomes firm.

When grains of corn are heated, the water and starch inside expand. They burst with a pop to create soft, fluffy popcorn.

Baking a cake

When we make a cake we often add baking powder to the cake mixture. This produces tiny bubbles of the gas carbon dioxide. In the oven, heat expands the bubbles and makes the cake mixture rise.

Bake some sponge cakes

Ask an adult to help you with this activity

You will need:

- fairy cake tin • margarine to grease the tin • 2 mixing bowls • electric whisk
- spoon • oven heated to gas mark 3/170°C

Mixture A 55 grams of plain flour, 1 egg, 55 grams of soft margarine, 55 grams of caster sugar

Mixture B 55 grams of plain flour, 1 teaspoon of baking powder, 1 egg, 55 grams of soft margarine, 55 grams of caster sugar

1 Lightly grease the fairy cake tin.

2 Put mixture A and mixture B (see above right) into two separate mixing bowls. Ask an adult to help you whisk the ingredients together.

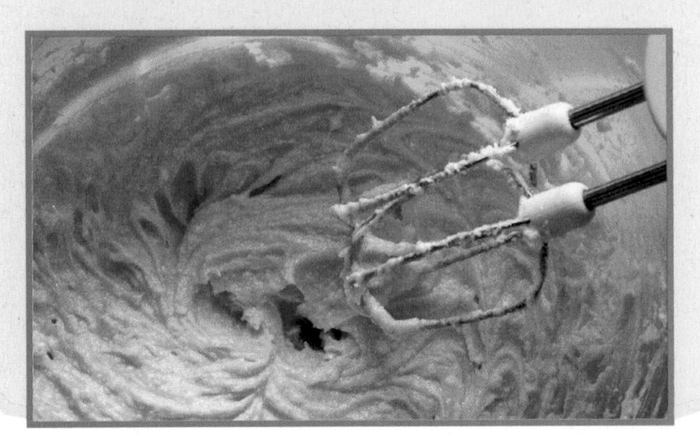

3 Fill half the fairy cake tin with mixture A, the other half with mixture B and bake in the centre of the oven for 15 to 20 minutes.

The mixture A cakes will look like flat biscuits while the mixture B cakes will have risen. The baking powder helps the cakes to rise.

Melt and mould

Some solid materials, such as glass and plastic, melt and become liquid when they are heated. They become solid again when they cool down. In the meantime, these materials can be melted and moulded into new shapes.

Moulding shapes

A mould is a container that gives the **molten** glass or plastic its shape. Plastic toys are made using moulds. When molten plastic is poured into a mould of a toy spaceship, for example, it hardens into a spaceship shape when it cools.

Rubber and plastic boots are moulded by machines in this factory.

Food

Butter, chocolate and cheese all melt when they are hot. A chocolate bar becomes soft and sticky on a warm day. Butter is easier to spread when it is warm than when taken straight from a cold fridge.

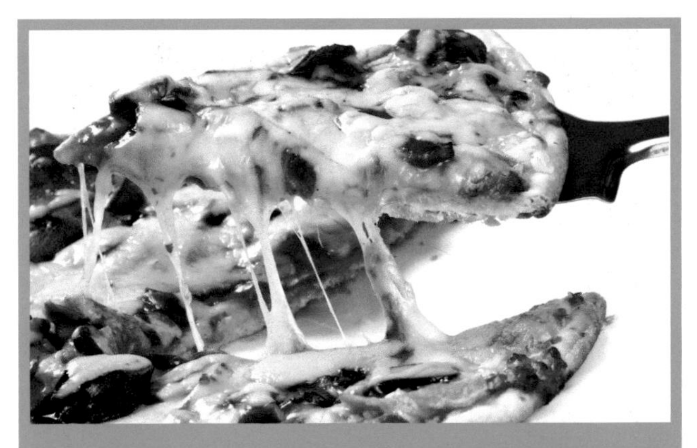

This pizza has been cooked in an oven. The cheese has melted.

Make chocolate shapes

Ask an adult to help you with this activity

You will need:
- bar of chocolate
- heatproof bowl
- saucepan
- water • baking tray
- pastry cutter shapes
- margarine • cake decorations (such as sugar strands)

1 Break the chocolate bar into pieces. Ask an adult to help you melt the chocolate in a bowl over a saucepan of simmering water.

2 Lightly grease a baking tray and the inside of some pastry cutter shapes.

3 Place the shapes on the tray and carefully pour in the melted chocolate.

4 Decorate and leave to cool.

Share the chocolate shapes with your friends!

Squash and stretch

You can squash and stretch some solid materials to change their shape. Clay is good for making models, for example. The clay keeps its new shape until it is squashed or stretched again.

Hardening

When soft, wet dough is baked in an oven, the heat changes it. It becomes firm and turns into bread. The only way to change its shape now is by tearing or cutting it.

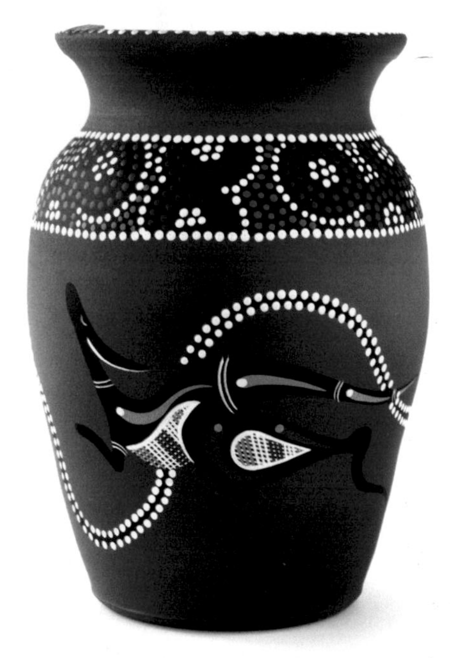

This woman is shaping soft, wet clay. When the pot is baked in a very hot oven, it can't be squashed and stretched again.

Elasticity

When some materials are stretched, their shape doesn't change for ever. These materials have **elasticity**. When you stretch rubber and elastic, for example, they snap back to their original shape when you let go.

Socks have elastic in them. They stretch when you put them on.

Make bouncing creatures

Ask an adult to help you with this activity

You will need:

- coloured card • coloured pens or pencils • scissors
- darning needle • sewing elastic (about 80 cm)
- beads (for weight)

1 Copy one of the animal shapes shown below onto the coloured card. Cut it out and decorate it.

2 Ask an adult to use the darning needle to pierce a hole through the middle of the body.

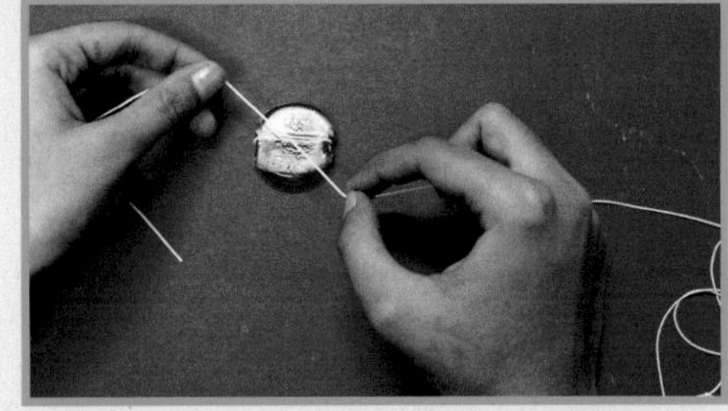

3 Tie one end of the sewing elastic to a big bead. Ask an adult to help you thread the other end through the hole, using a darning needle, from the underside of the body.

4 Bounce your creature up and down on the sewing elastic.

Recycling materials

We often use things and throw them away when we have finished with them. Instead of wasting the materials they are made of, it makes sense to use them to make something else.

Saving resources

Recycling means to break something down and use the materials to make something new. Many materials, such as paper, plastic, glass and metal, can be recycled. Recycling helps to save **resources**.

Paper is made from wood. Recycling paper can save trees from being cut down.

Biodegradable plastic bags rot into the soil with this garden rubbish.

Natural materials

Biodegradable materials, such as paper and cotton, break down naturally and become part of the soil, water or air. Some plastics are now made to be biodegradable.

Make and recycle paper

Ask an adult to help you with this activity

You will need:

- used paper
- bowl of warm water
- egg beater
- rectangle of fine mesh (from your local hardware store or garden centre)
- tray
- 2 large sheets of blotting paper
- electric iron

1 Tear the paper into small pieces and put them in a bowl of warm water. Leave to soak for a few minutes.

2 Ask an adult to help you beat the mixture with an egg beater to make a pulp.

3 Put the mesh into the tray. Pour the pulp onto the mesh and smooth it into a thin layer. Leave to drain.

4 Turn the mesh onto a sheet of blotting paper. Cover it with the other sheet of blotting paper. Ask an adult to help you press it with a warm iron.

5 Lift off the top sheet of blotting paper. When it has dried out thoroughly, you can use your paper.

Modern materials

People have always made things from the materials they find around them – from stone and wood to grass and soil. Now, many new materials have been created for special uses.

Racing cars

The first racing cars were made of heavy metal. This slowed them down. Today, racing cars are made of a new material called **carbon fibre**. It is strong and light and good for racing at high speed.

Modern racing cars made of carbon fibre move faster than older racing cars made of heavy metal.

Kevlar®

Kevlar® is another very strong, light material. It is made from a type of plastic, called nylon, and is used to make helmets and body armour. It is much lighter and quieter than the heavy metal armour worn by knights long ago!

Strong, light materials make it easy for these soldiers to move quickly and quietly.

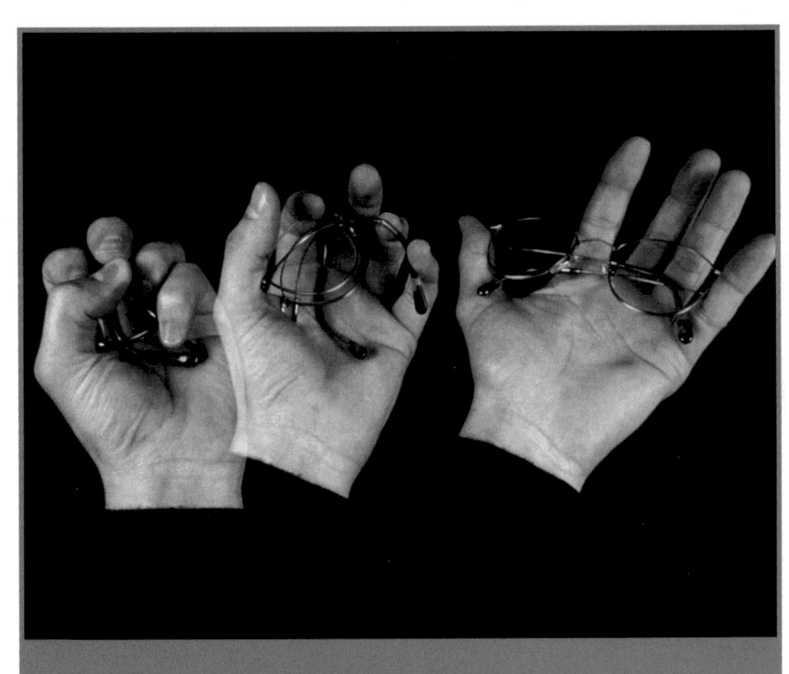

A memory metal helps to keep the shape of the frames of these glasses, even when they are bent or twisted.

Smart materials

New materials are being developed called **smart materials**. They can sense conditions around them and change if necessary. Memory metal, for example, is a smart material that 'remembers' the shape it has been given. Memory metal is a good material for glasses frames that might get bent or twisted.

Glossary

absorbent
Materials that are absorbent soak up or take in liquid. A sponge is made of absorbent material.

biodegradable
Biodegradable materials break down or decay naturally and become part of the soil, water or air.

boil
Liquids boil when they are heated to a high temperature. At their boiling point, they start to bubble and turn into gas.

carbon dioxide
Carbon dioxide is a gas in the air. We breathe out carbon dioxide and plants take it in. When fuels are burned, they give out carbon dioxide.

carbon fibre
Carbon fibre is a strong, light thread used to make other materials, such as metal, stronger.

dissolve
When a solid dissolves in a liquid, it becomes absorbed and makes a solution.

elasticity
Materials with elasticity can be stretched, pulled or squashed and will snap back to their original shape or size.

evaporate
A liquid evaporates when it is heated, and changes into water vapour.

expand
When a material expands, it spreads out and becomes larger.

freeze
When liquids reach a low enough temperature, they freeze and become solid. This temperature is called the freezing point.

limestone
Limestone is a type of rock.

melt
When some solids are heated, they melt and become liquid. The temperature is called the melting point.

mixture
A mixture contains different substances mixed together. You mix ingredients to make cake mixture, for example.

molten
Solids become molten when they are heated and melt into a liquid.

moulded
Solids are moulded by being melted, poured into a mould and then left to cool and harden into the shape of the mould.

polystyrene foam
Polystyrene foam is a type of light plastic filled with bubbles of air.

properties
A material's properties describe what it is like.

resources
Resources are supplies of the things we use, such as metal, oil or coal.

smart materials
Smart materials are made to sense what is going on around them and to change if necessary.

solution
A solution is made when a substance mixes with a liquid and dissolves completely.

stalactite
A stalactite is an icicle-shaped pillar hanging down from the roof of a cave, formed when minerals in dripping water are left behind.

stalagmite
Stalagmites are formed in the same way as stalactites. They grow up from the cave floor.

waterproof
Waterproof materials do not absorb or soak up water.

Index